M000077994

WRITING
in
BULLETS

WRITING
in
BULLETS

The New Rules for Maximum
Business Communication

by Kim Long

RUNNING PRESS
PHILADELPHIA • LONDON

© 2003 by Kim Long
All rights reserved under the Pan-American and
International Copyright Conventions
Printed in the United States

*This book may not be reproduced in whole or in part, in any form or by
any means, electronic or mechanical, including photocopying, record-
ing, or by any information storage and retrieval system now known or
hereafter invented, without written permission from the publisher.*

9   8   7   6   5   4   3   2   1
Digit on the right indicates the number of this printing

Library of Congress Control Number 2003108872

ISBN 0-7624-1597-5

Cover design by Whitney Cookman
Interior design by Kim Long
Edited by Greg Jones
Typography: Goudy Old Style

This book may be ordered by mail from the publisher.
Please include $2.50 for postage and handling.
But try your bookstore first!

Running Press Book Publishers
125 South Twenty-second Street
Philadelphia, Pennsylvania 19103-4399

Visit us on the Web!
www.runningpress.com

Contents

Acknowledgements

Special thanks to individuals and organizations assisting in this project:

Dr. Bill Casey and Wendy Peck,
Executive Leadership Group, Inc.

Gregory McNamee

Dr. Randall Lockwood

Pat Wagner and Leif Smith, Pattern Research

Kathleen Cain,
Front Range Community College

Tom Auer and Marilyn Auer,
The Bloomsbury Review

Steve Elliott, Forethought Media

Introduction

With the exception of diaries, which people write primarily for themselves, writing is a medium intended for communication. This may be communication between only two people or many, a known audience or an anonymous one, but no matter who sees it, in order for the writing to communicate effectively, it must permit ideas, facts, and intention to be transmitted appropriately. No confusion, no wasted time, no wasted effort.

But there are fundamental differences in the kinds of writing and who the writing is intended for. A poem written for a lover has different style and content requirements than a definition written for a dictionary. In today's fast-paced, competitive business environment, writing also may have different roles depending on what it is intended to accomplish. An executive summary is different from an owner's manual; a resume different from a business plan.

Yet most contemporary uses of nonfiction prose do share some similarities, especially if clear information delivery is the goal. Published text in all formats has to compete in a rising sea of information; information overload is a reality and forces readers to make choices about what to read. Shorter text is not possible nor desirable in many cases, but especially in business and academic writing, it is critical to cut through the increasing clutter. This goal creates an important role for short, concise writing, but this brevity requires care.

The substitution of conclusions and condensed abstracts for complete disclosure of information opens a can of worms for the average writer. The fewer the words, the harder the writing. This is where lists and bulleted items provide an ideal bridge.

Not every chunk of prose should or can be reduced to a bulleted list. The Gettysburg Address is one spectacular example, unimprovable through condensation. The Ten Commandments, on the other hand, is the equivalent of a bulleted list in its original form in The Bible, unimprovable through expansion.

To write a well-turned bulleted list is somewhere between rule-governed craft and instinct-guided art. The outcome benefits from following standard, consistent guidelines but it only works well when the content is expressed with the right style.

The material presented here was created from several decades of writing and publishing experience. Some guidelines are simple and even obvious extensions of writing conventions that have been in use long before the advent of word processors and the Internet; basic elements of style change little over time. But the appearance of text on computer monitors, Web pages, and in digital slide presentations — all part of the modern environment of business writing — has added new criteria for writers.

The result may be a process that is a little more complicated, but the outcome can also be more effective and reach audiences more directly than in the pre-computer era. Some of the new guidelines added here are based on recent laboratory research measuring human reactions to type, text, and digital images, objective knowledge that can add value to written content produced for communication with others.

Additional guidelines presented here come from experts working in the field of personal and corporate communications, representing how written material actually is used — and abused — in the business world.

What Is a Bullet?

- *In publishing circles, a "bullet" is a small graphic symbol used in front of a block of type to help set it apart from other text.*

Despite the connection between the shape and the word, the term bullet for these type elements is recent, dating to about the 1950s. Yet the little devices go back much farther, appearing in hand-written illuminated manuscripts in the Middle Ages, long before printing presses and printing type showed up. Some sources also point to bullet-like elements used in some ancient Egyptian hieroglyphics.

In early forms of printing, paragraphs were a missing feature and text was run on without breaks. In their place were small graphic figures that formed the same purpose as paragraph indents do today, making it easier to read a large block of text by breaking it into more visually distinct segments. The term for such a paragraph marker was *pilcrow* — its modern equivalent is the ¶ sign — and it inspired the use of other type symbols to embellish, highlight, or decorate printed material.

Typesetters used the word *fleuron* (or *floret*) to refer to these symbols, terms used in English by the 1600s. In the original context in French, these words both mean "flower," an apt term as the first designs looked like small flowers — ❀ is one example. The fleuron is the ancestor of the bullet, although fleurons were mostly used for decoration, not to emphasize text.

The English word bullet was borrowed from French in the early 1500s, where it was originally *boule*, meaning "ball." From *boule* came *boulet* to refer to cannonballs, and from *boulet* came *boulette* to refer to small cannonballs or the even smaller round ammunition used in hand-held firearms. The word was borrowed for use in typesetting because some fleurons were simple round dots, evoking the image of such ammunition.

In modern typesetting terminology, bullets are part of a group called *pi characters* — most commonly referred to as dingbats — which include various signs, symbols, and marks supplementing the regular alphabet. These days, bullets are referred to with different terms. English synonyms include bug, chip, and ball, each suggesting the form of a real object, just as bullet does itself.

Bullet Variety

Type collections provide a rich variety of bullet designs, many available for use in word processors and desktop publishing. For almost all business use, these graphic choices are unnecessary, distracting, and too cute. Stick to the basics: the ● or the ■.

Why Use Bullets?

- *Bulleted text focuses attention, organizes content, and simplifies conclusions.*

Text is a basic form of communication. Its effectiveness depends on content, style, and method of delivery, most of which the writer controls. The addition of bullets to text is not the most important factor, nor the least, but a useful element in improving this communication form.

Bullets perform a multitude of valuable functions. They can be used to:

- segregate information
- focus attention
- add structure to layouts
- organize content
- simplify conclusions
- emphasize main points

Especially in an era marked by "information overload," bullets are a considerable aid in the condensation of text. Used on Web pages, slide presentations, or printed documents, bulleted material helps focus reader attention, reduce tedium, and improve comprehension.

In an increasing array of business applications, bulleted lists are a desirable, if not mandatory, style for published text. But using them effectively should not be automatic; they are not a magic solution to every writing project. In fact, automated, formulaic, and unthinking use of bullets may contribute to the opposite effect, turning this practical tool into a bore, a predictable audience turn-off.

Basic decisions about usage include the targeting of text to be bulleted, layout and design related to the bullets and lists used, and the refining of list text to improve its effectiveness, not to mention the need to keep an eye out for overuse.

The Hybrid Writer

- *Effective use of bullets and lists requires a combination of writing and design decisions.*

Traditionally, writers have been responsible for creating text and designers have been responsible for its appearance on a page. But in the modern era of word processors — and heavy emphasis on writing styles for presentations in overhead transparencies, PowerPoint presentations, and Web pages — the role of the writer has expanded to include decisions about layout, type fonts, and other elements of design, options only a few keystrokes away.

The use of bullets and lists is part of this hybrid writing/design application. Writers themselves make decisions about the use of their text in the new formats, and they often have to deal with options that far exceed the limited variables connected to the typewriter, the predecessor of the personal computer.

Not only do Web pages and slide presentations demand more design decisions, traditional document formats also now have expanded design elements, primarily because of laser and inkjet printers. All of these greatly exceed the design range of typewriters. With both the old and new formats, however, the goal remains the same: effective communication.

Writers who have knowledge of and control over design in addition to command of the language will increase their prose power. Plus, in many of today's business environments, whoever writes the prose is also often saddled with the task of producing it in final form. Design decisions are now an essential part of many job functions. And especially with the demands generated by bullets and lists, knowledge of design as well as writing style adds control and power at the creative end.

Bullet Basics

- *The visual appearance of bullets affects the impact of the text they accompany.*

The selection of a bullet style may seem daunting, given the hundreds of choices available. They are available within most font sets and dozens of specialty font sets provide many additional designs, including symbols meant for professional applications and those meant merely as amusing decoration. On the Web, unique bullet styles have also appeared for use in lists in this environment.

The basic steps for bullet use are:
- Selection   • Size   • Alignment
- Spacing   • Centering

Bullet Selection

In business as in life, simpler is better. Unless there is a compelling reason to use a specialized bullet for a specific application, stick with the basics: the round ● or the square ■.

How do you find a bullet character? In Microsoft Windows, open the utility called Character Map and use the font menu to select the font you are using. The "map" is a graphic layout of every character included with each font set — including upper and lower case letters, numerals, and punctuation marks — each represented in the same position on the map.

The Character Map utility allows you to highlight a particular character and copy it, from which it can be pasted into your text wherever the cursor is positioned. The ● character is on the fourth row, eleventh position in from the right. You can also pop this character directly into the text with a keyboard shortcut.

Activate the Character Map utility with this menu sequence: Start/Programs/Accessories. In some windows systems, the file may be at: Start/Programs/ Accessories/System Tools. Or search for "charmap.exe" and double-click on the file name.

Shortcut: Press and hold the ALT key while typing the numerals 0149 on the number pad.

Once the bullet has been inserted and sized, use the copy and paste functions to add more of the same wherever they are need in the text. The copy and paste functions can also transfer other bullet characteristics, such as size and spacing, reducing the need to repeat these tasks.

Fonts such as Wingdings and Zapf Dingbats also include basic bullets, but these fonts require a little more work. First type a lower case "l" where you want the bullet to be, then highlight this character and use the pull-down menu to change the font to either of these.

l becomes ● in Zapf Dingbats and ● in Wingdings.
m becomes ○ in Zapf Dingbats and ○ in Wingdings.
n becomes ■ in Zapf Dingbats and ■ in Wingdings.
o becomes ❑ in Zapf Dingbats and ❑ in Wingdings.

These programs generate the bullet in a larger size than the text font bullet, requiring adjustment down in size.

The quick and dirty way to add bullets to a list is to use a utility to do the work for you. All major word processing programs include this feature. In Microsoft Word or PowerPoint, highlight the targeted list and open **Bullets & Numbering** in the **Format** menu. Seven simple bullet styles and layout options are offered, and a **Customize**

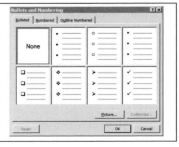

A format tool in Word and PowerPoint adds bullets or numbers to a list, with preselected bullet and layout styles.

feature allows you to control selections further.

The biggest flaw with the feature, however, is the lack of control over spacing between the bullets and the list entries. The default selection produces more space than is necessary, but if you can live with the appearance, the ease of use makes this a valuable asset.

Bullet Size

The size of bullets should relate to the size of the type used in list entries. As a general rule, bullets should neither overwhelm the lists they serve nor be underwhelmed by nearby type. This can be a delicate balancing act, but the results are worth the effort.

In most printed text, type sizes of 10 to 12 points are standard and should also apply to bulleted material. For overhead transparencies or other slide presentations such as PowerPoint or Keynote where material is projected for an audience, use 30 to 34 point type.

Web pages fall somewhat in between. Use 12 to 14 point type for most text, including bulleted lists, unless the material is shorter and is targeted for special treatment, in which case slightly larger type can be used.

If you use the standard round bullet that comes with most fonts, it usually looks best one or two point sizes less than the rest of the text.

THIS WAY:	NOT THIS WAY:	OR THIS WAY:
• fax	● fax	· fax
• email	● email	· email
• telephone	● telephone	· telephone

10 point bullet • 11 point type
11 point bullet • 12 point type
12 point bullet • 13 point type
13 point bullet • 14 point type
14 point bullet • 15 point type

Bullet Alignment

Keep bullets in a vertical line. This reduces visual confusion and helps set the bulleted list apart from other text.

THIS WAY	NOT THIS WAY
• Kansas City	• Kansas City
• Nashville	• Nashville
• Chicago	• Chicago

Bullet Spacing

The power of bullets to set text apart can be diminished if the bullets are placed too close to the list text. Add at least one extra space between a bullet and an entry. Too much space, however, and the entries appear too separated from the bullets they are supposed to be attached to.

THIS WAY	NOT THIS WAY	OR THIS WAY
• Executives	•Executives	• Executives
• Managers	•Managers	• Managers
• Employees	•Employees	• Employees

Bullet Centering

Best spot for the bullet: centered at half the height of a lowercase letter. Entries with more than one line of text should have the bullet centered on the first line. When first popped into the text, bullets are often placed too high or too low in their default position, but this can be easily adjusted. In Microsoft Word, the tool for adjusting height is in the **Format Menu** under **Font**. Select the tab marked **Character Spacing**, and the **Position** adjustment to raise or lower the bullet. A shift of only 1 or 2 points (use the hyphen or minus key in front of a number to indicate a downward shift) is usually all that is necessary.

THIS WAY	NOT THIS WAY	OR THIS WAY
• Planning	• Planning	• Planning
• Research	• Research	• Research
• Testing	• Testing	• Testing

The most effective vertical position for a bullet is a placement halfway between the top and bottom of a lowercase letter that has no ascenders or descenders (referred to as the x-height).

The most effective horizontal position for a bullet is about one or two spaces in front of a list entry.

18

Bulleted List Layout

- *Careful attention to left and right margins will enhance the effectiveness of bulleted lists.*

The Left Margin

Other than the bullets, the main factor that sets a list apart from surrounding text is the left margin. A list can stand out merely by being inset from the surrounding text, but bullets are essential as 'stop points,' graphic elements that cause readers' eyes to momentarily focus on a fixed position while they are scanning.

Many lists are used without any surrounding text, as in PowerPoint presentations and Web sites, where the left margin is less critical. But when used inside of a text document, the left margin position — carefully chosen — improves comprehension of the intended material.

Traditionally, bulleted lists were often lined up on the left margin even with the text blocks above and below. This position works but can be improved, especially when a list consists of short entries, by shifting the entire list to the right. With short entries, any inset amount improves the overall look. The target: 0.25" to 0.50".

Too much space on the left margin, however, may make lists appear downright peculiar. What is too much? Half the width of the normal text is too much and one third is about the maximum. Lists that include sub-lists should follow the visual pattern set by the original inset, making the inset list offset by the same or a lesser amount.

RULE OF THUMB	Adjust a list's left margin to allow the items in the list to run on a single line each or the same number of lines per entry.

> A bulleted list placed within a page of regular text makes a better impression when it is inset from the existing margin.

Online Migration

Year by year, the Internet has made a bigger impact on B2B activity, providing more applications and solutions and attracting more users. From business analytics to electronic invoicing, the wide-ranging network has proven an appropriate way to improve productivity and reduce costs. Trends in online invoicing now include a push to standardization and use of existing software formats already in wide use in financial software and database applications.

Security issues here are also critical, but less important than in consumer applications because businesses — especially large enterprises — are better able to control and limit communications between vendors, suppliers, clients, and the "outside world."

Another trend is integration, with interactive links between online business applications and company-wide users, databases, and business partners. Spending on e-business applications has been robust in recent years as businesses prepare for the next generation of activity, but the recession did dampen spending in this area, at least temporarily. Top factors cited by executives for investing in e-business initiatives in 2001:

- cost reduction
- improved customer support
- improved customer retention
- increased efficiency
- increased market share
- increased return on investment (AMR)

One change already underway in B2B action online is a de-emphasis in market-based exchanges, with demand building for private exchanges instead. In 2001, about 12 percent of major U.S. corporations used private exchanges; participation in public exchanges was also about 12 percent. But the former application is on the rise, while the latter is fading in favor, at least according to some analysts.

Never center the entries in a list. Centering is an appropriate option for titles, not for text, because it is more difficult to read from one line to another.

The Right Margin

A ragged right margin is the best option for lists. If list lines are justified (forced to an exact width), the words in the entries are likely to be skewed, stretched, or awkwardly placed. Justification typically creates a mess with short lines of text.

If a right margin is used, reduce it slightly from that set for the regular text. This helps keep the list material visually distinct when the list contents consist of longer entries, those that run longer than one line each. The right margin inset for a list should be the same or less than that used for the left margin.

Entry with right margin even with text:
- 51 percent of business email users check for mail at least once per hour.

Same entry with added right margin:
- 51 percent of business email users check for mail at least once per hour.

Line Spacing

Line spacing is a key factor in readability. For blocks of text used in normal printed material, the optimum line spacing — called "leading" in traditional typesetting — is 1 or 2 points more than the type size.

For 11 point type, for example, this means line spacing of 12 (11 + 1) to 13 (11 + 2), or a position halfway, 12 1/2 (11 + 1 1/2). This setting is often the default in word processing programs and is acceptable in most situations. But if a little extra space is desirable, a lot is not. Too much leading in regular text decreases readability because the eye is slower to "track" from the end of one line to the beginning of another.

Lists should be managed differently from regular text. Even though a list is already set apart visually from the surrounding text, it is more distinctive when extra line spacing is added between entries.

The most effective way to do this is to leave the line spacing setting at its fixed measurement and use the **format** or **paragraph** menu control to add extra space after each entry. Add 0.02" to 0.05" after each line.

REGULAR LINE SPACING

- soft drinks $60 billion
- spirits $37 billion
- beer $19 billion
- juice $12 billion
- bottled water $5 billion
- wine $5 billion

ADDED LINE SPACING

- soft drinks $60 billion
- spirits $37 billion
- beer $19 billion
- juice $12 billion
- bottled water $5 billion
- wine $5 billion

RECOMMENDED SPACING   EXCESSIVE SPACING

11 pt type + 0.03"

- revenue $118 billion
- expenses $110 billion
- net profit $8 billion
- profit margin 4.7 percent

11 pt type + 0.05"

- revenue $118 billion
- expenses $110 billion
- net profit $8 billion
- profit margin 4.7 percent

11 pt type + 0.15"

- revenue $118 billion
- expenses $110 billion
- net profit $8 billion
- profit margin 4.7 percent

Additional line spacing changes enhance lists even more. Before and after a list or its headline, this extra space helps the eye separate it from adjacent text blocks.

No added line space after title:

College Enrollment Changes

total students	+7 percent
part-time students	+1 percent
full-time students	+14 percent

Added line space after title:

College Enrollment Changes

total students	+7 percent
part-time students	+1 percent
full-time students	+14 percent

Capitalization

In most cases, begin bullet entries with a capital letter. This helps separate entries visually, makes each one distinct from the others, and helps visually emphasize the list as an organized set of information.

But this is not a hard and fast rule. Sometimes, a bulleted list may look better when entries begin with lower-case letters, as in lists made up of single words or short phrases. Another exception is when list entries are words or phrases in a series following the list title or lead-in, as in the following example.

Office design trends include:

- personalized workspaces
- ergonomic interfaces
- wireless communications links
- accommodations for older workers

In this kind of series, unlike in regular text, there is no need to add commas or semi-colons after each entry or insert an "and" before the last entry.

One important guideline with capitalization is consistency. If you begin one entry with a capital letter, do the same with all entries in the same list and all lists in the same document. And watch out for the same errors that are linked to the misuse of capitals in regular text. For example, always use a capital letter to begin a proper name.

The one hard rule for capital letters: *Never use all caps for an entire entry or list.* In this case, the caps create a barrier to readability. During the process of reading, the smooth horizontal flow of eye movement is reinforced by the variation in the tops of letters as they are used in lower-case versions. This variation is directly linked to the efficiency with which the human brain processes words. The process works most efficiently with lower-case letters because their variation helps the brain recognize familiar letter groups faster and more accurately; when the tops of letters are all at the same height — as in a row of capital letters — reading speed slows down.

Which style is easier to read?

Corporate benefits:	**Corporate benefits:**
• Food service	• FOOD SERVICE
• Exercise facilities	• EXERCISE FACILITIES
• Legal assistance	• LEGAL ASSISTANCE

Bold & Italic

Regular text can be enhanced by using bold and italic to highlight words. Just as with bullets, bold and italic words create 'stop points' that cause eyes to momentarily pause, an effective way to add emphasis. Use this practic sparingly in lists, however, as overuse makes text appear cluttered, diluting the effect.

In general, use bold or italic for only one or two words per entry. Typically, you should not use this format on an entire entry or list. Why? The same research that determined the use of all caps slows down reading speed reports the same results when large chunks of text are in a bold or italic style.

Airport shuttle changes:

- Rental car companies will increasingly **consolidate services.**
- More rental car facilities will shift to **remote facilities.**
- Shuttle vehicles will switch to **alternative fuels** to reduce pollution near airport terminals.

Punctuation

The first application of punctuation in a list is with the list title or introduction. In most cases, a title or lead-in is distinctive enough to be used without punctuation at all, especially if the type here is larger or bolder than the list that follows. If punctuation is used, a colon is the preferred form.

Avoid using a comma or semi-colon after a lead-in sentence or phrase. A comma is ambiguous and does not provide an appropriate visual break and the semi-colon has a specific role that does not include preceding a group or list of items.

An ellipses (...) can also be used, as well as a long dash (traditionally called an em dash, —). Avoid using a hyphen, however, as it does not provide much of a visual mark. The ellipses has traditionally been used within text to indicate missing or skipped material, not to indicate the beginning of a series, but in the evolving world of English this former use is expanding and it may be used as a substitute for the colon.

Variations for lead-in phrases for lists:

Applications for digital technology in houses:

Applications for digital technology in houses ...

Applications for digital technology in houses —

In the list itself, the end of each entry also provides an opportunity for punctuation. But list entries that are single words or phrases do not require any punctuation. Sentences and paragraphs used as list entries should be ended with a period.

The major consideration is consistency. Use the same punctuation — or none — for each entry in the same list and each list in the same publication. In general, entries that begin with a capital letter can be completed with a period and entries that begin in lower-case letters — phrases, other incomplete sentences, or single words — should not end in periods.

This way:

- Snowboarding.
- Cross-country skiing.
- Downhill skiing.

Not this way:

- snowboarding.
- cross-country skiing.
- downhill skiing.

When phrases are used as list entries to complete an introductory line, they should be entered without a capital letter and should not have a comma, semi-colon, or period at the end of each item. These punctuation marks are used in regular text out of necessity to make each item visually distinct but in a list, the structure already performs this function.

A successful board member is able to ...

- influence others
- solve problems
- think about the future

Hyphenation

Readability in lists is improved if there are few or no hyphens. This is because list items are typically short and short lines of text are unnecessarily broken up with hyphenization. Hyphenization can be controlled in word processing programs by selecting the **no hyphens** option or removing them by adding space in the right margin.

Hyphens are not a critical element, however, and their use may actually be beneficial when list entries are long or technical terms require splitting to fit. In some cases, hyphens can be dropped for all list entries except where one may help break a long word. As a rule, hyphenation should not be used on proper names.

With hyphens:

Changes in second-home ownership:

- More contractors and realtors specializing in this ownership segment.
- Expanding target for sales of housewares, furnishings, and appliances.
- Evolution of vacation sites from seasonal to year-round communities.
- Increasing use by owners for work, with requirements for high-speed Internet access.

Without hyphens:

Changes in second-home ownership:

- More contractors and realtors specializing in this ownership segment.
- Expanding target for sales of housewares, furnishings, and appliances.
- Evolution of vacation sites from seasonal to year-round communities.
- Increasing use by owners for work, with requirements for high-speed Internet access.

Overkill

- *Too many bullets reduce the effectiveness of bullets.*

The right amount of bulleted material adds structure to a document or presentation and facilitates communication. Too many bullets, on the other hand, create the reverse effect, as does the use of overly decorative bullets or those that are overly large. A bullet-heavy document can appear too busy or too thin in substance, scattering attention rather than focusing it. The worst case scenario: bored or annoyed readers.

A slide presentation may consist only of bulleted items and perform its mission perfectly well, however, because in this medium, the presenter controls the pace of the presentation. Only a single slide's worth of text is viewed at a time. Plus, these kinds of presentations are typically short, intended to provide highlights, summaries, and conclusions, all conducive to the bulleted style. Even so, slide presentations are often more effective when graphs, charts, and other graphic elements are altered with bulleted lists.

In printed text, information is processed in discrete chunks, with the readers' eyes scanning material at a consistent speed. Headlines, italicized or bold-faced text, and bullets interrupt this flow with 'stop points' that focus attention by momentarily interrupting this scanning action. Underlining and the use of color also produce this effect.

'Stop points' are valuable tools when deliberately deployed to attract and focus attention. But if too many are on a page or throughout a publication, the impact of any one targeted element is diluted. Not to mention that readers may suffer eye fatigue, a physiological side effect generated by some kinds of text. Negative effects also crop up if there is too much variation in type fonts, type size, or type color on one page, slide, or Web screen. Excessive variation does not enhance a display, it creates a visual mess. Pick a simple bullet style and stick with it throughout a document or presentation.

RULE OF THUMB
Avoid Bullet Overkill

- Limit bullet list length to six or fewer items (exceptions are acceptable if necessary, as in this list).

- Use color sparingly. One additional color is enough for most uses in bulleted lists.

- Use type fonts sparingly. One type for text and one for headlines is adequate.

- Use no more than one bulleted list per page in printed documents (with opposing pages, one per page spread).

- Limit bullet lists on Web pages to no more than one per screen.

- The shorter the list entries, the fewer entries per list. Lists with one- or two-word entries should generally not exceed five or six items.

- Use a graph or chart instead of a list when possible.

- Don't add bullets to centered headlines or labels.

- Don't use a bullet in combination with indented text. One or the other is all that is necessary.

A Menu of Lists

- *Lists can be segregated into various types based on their elements.*

Entries in a list can consist of single words, phrases, sentences, or paragraphs, and represent ideas, facts, changes, or many other kinds of information. Each type represents unique opportunities to improve the flow of communication with the intended audience by using an appropriate format.

Each list should have its own consistency, with each entry roughly parallel in structure to the others. In other words, don't mix sentences with single words from entry to entry in the same list. On the other hand, you can use more than one kind of list in the same document, selecting the appropriate style to match the need.

Companies and organizations often have internal guidelines about publication formats — including bulleted lists — but even when the rules limit the options, the writer can improve the results. One of the most critical factors is the logic used to target and organize the list contents.

In every list, there is a reason why the contents have value and this reason can be directly linked to the logic used to organize it. The contents are either balanced in value, or represent a definitive order.

Organization methods for lists include:

• alphabetic	• chronological
• geographical	• step-by-step
• numerical value	• supporting evidence
• persuasive order	• equal value (no ranking)
• relative importance or priority	

Data Lists

Among all forms of information, data may benefit most from the list structure. When numbers or facts are lined up, organized, or outlined in this distinctive manner, individual figures are easier to pick out and comparisons are more obvious. This improves the reader's interpretation of the information.

But numbers can also be numbing when listed. Other formats — graphs and charts, for example — can be more effective than bulleted lists. The first task when selecting data for presentation is to determine the most appropriate format. Existing patterns of usage within an organization are a useful guide in this determination, but a general rule

---

Data in bulleted list format:

Longevity of stores in shopping centers:

- 12 percent   open more than 20 years
- 25 percent   open 11-20 years
- 33 percent   open 6-10 years
- 14 percent   open 3-5 years
- 5 percent   open 2 years or less

Is this information easier to understand in another format?

20+ years
11–20 years
6–10 years
3–5 years
2 years or less

When list information requires two columns, the entries are more difficult to read if the columns are too close together or too far apart. Position the second column so that there is 0.2" to 0.5" of space between the longest line in the first column and the leading edge of the second.

Highest rates of uninsured residents:

- New Mexico   22.6 percent
- Texas   22.2 percent
- Arizona, Louisiana   19.5 percent
- Montana   18.3 percent
- Alaska   18.1 percent

of thumb is to only use a bulleted list for data if there are fewer than six entries. Also use a chart if the information requires three or more columns.

Data in bulleted lists typically follows some kind of organization. Entries are ranked or grouped according to a specific logic, highest to lowest, for example. Entries listed randomly are vulnerable to misreading because human minds are "hard-wired" to make sense out of new information. This is done through the recognition of patterns, whether one is intended or not. Avoid such accidents with careful organization and appropriate labeling.

When numbers are the primary element in a data list, the list will improve visually if the numbers are lined up, either along their right edge or by using the decimal point or "," as the anchor point. For the sake of consistency, keep the form of each entry the same, using the same number of decimal places, for example. When there is a mixed set of numbers — some whole, some fractions, for example — align them along their left edge.

Research has shown that numbers are easier to process mentally — and remember — if they are in groups of one to four digits. Commas or spaces should be used in longer numbers in order to generate this grouping. Rounding up or down is also effective in reducing awkward-looking entries, and large numbers can benefit from the use of words to replace standard units.

This: 35,700   Instead of: 35700

This: 35,000   Instead of: 35,099

This: 183 million   Instead of: 183,000,000

When numbers are used alone in a list — without key words or defining terms after the number — make sure to include a defining term in the title or lead-in line, representing the basic unit of measurement. Is it dollars, percent, tons, millions of miles? And in numbers-only lists, the use of periods at the end of each entry is unnecessary and adds unwanted visual clutter.

Data presented in lists should have clear explanatory text that allows readers to grasp intention and avoid incorrect assumptions.

Recent Trends in Domestic Travel

- business travel   *up 2 percent*
- pleasure travel   *up 1 percent*
- business travel with children   *up 19 percent*
- pleasure travel with children   *up 9 percent*
- solo business travel   *down 1 percent*
- solo pleasure travel   *down 6 percent*

Word or Phrase Lists

In this style, the short nature of each entry heightens the importance of organization. Does one item come first or do all represent equal value? Also, visual cues are more prominent here, making it critical to line up margins and align key components.

When single words are used as list entries, pay attention to factors which influence their placement within the list. If there is no special order intended, make sure that no order is implied accidentally.

Enhance message content with:
- Repetition
- Visualization
- Structure
- Readability

Fastest growing segments for home sales:
- Active adults
- Single buyers
- Second homes

Major project stages
- Design
- Manufacturing
- Testing
- Evaluation

Sentence Lists

Sentences do not have to be avoided in lists, even when the goal is to make entries short, but sentence length is an important issue. The shorter the sentence, the quicker it delivers a message. Sentence length can be offset, however, by shortening the line length. The shorter the line, the greater the readability. Concise writing, summarized content, and shorter line lengths can make sentence lists more effective.

When sentence entries are long, line length can be controlled by adjusting both the left and right margins. The target on an average document page should be 50 to 75 percent fewer words per line than the surrounding text, or about four to six words in general. Also use the margin adjustment to avoid awkward-looking line breaks,

---

Sentence list with full line length:

- Consumer software lets customers comparison shop.
- Price-checking software allows retailers to keep track of competitors.
- Online-pricing software automates price adjustments.

Sentence list with shorter line length
(right margin set in 0.5"):

- Consumer software allows customers to comparison shop.
- Price-checking software allows retailers to keep track of competitors.
- Online-pricing software automates price adjustments.

---

such as those that leave a single, short word by itself on a line. Another approach for sentence entries is to use sub-heads for each entry in a leading column. This method speeds up comprehension if the subhead summarizes the content of each entry.

The key rule of sentence use in lists is consistency, with each following the same logic of use. The placement of nouns and verbs, verb tense, and use of modifiers must be parallel, with these key words in the same position in each entry. Another, less critical goal, is to make the length of each entry match as much as possible. The toughest task here is list entries that vary from one to many lines per entry, producing a visually-awkward construction.

Hyphens are best avoided in sentence lists, but they can also be used to fix awkward-looking layouts. However, watch out for single words or syllables orphaned on the last line, a situation that is not favorable. If this occurs, adjust the right margin slightly until the orphaned objects go away.

Using sub-heads in a sentence list:

- **Size**   Sites are getting larger because of increased demand and physically larger RVs.

- **Market**   Distinct groups of consumers have created new demand for specialized sites based on demographic and cultural traits.

- **Location**   Proximity to an urban center is a driving factor in the success of new sites.

Paragraph Lists

Paragraphs are the most difficult text element to deal with in lists. Their bulk works against the condensed nature of the list itself, but design options can make them work effectively nevertheless.

If list entries must run longer than one sentence per entry, use standard writing and editing applications to make them as concise as possible. The design of paragraph lists also benefits from extra care paid to the margins and buffer spacing between the list and surrounding text, generating more visual clues to distinguish between the two.

In general, paragraph entries become more readable when the line length is reduced. This is controlled by

Paragraph list sample:

- Music sales and distribution are migrating to the Internet, but the shift comes at a cost to record companies. Our service enables record labels to offset this cost.

- Record companies will evolve to take greater advantage of digital music, adapting new processes and methods to make this move. Our new service provides powerful tools to help record companies move to the digital model.

- Digital music presents unique dangers to record companies, reducing their control over the products they distribute. Our new service reverses this trend, placing control back in the lap of the record companies.

increasing the left margin and/or adding a right margin to the existing value set for surrounding text. A figure of 0.3" to 0.5" works well. If the margins are shifted, maintain the same settings throughout a document.

If possible, make each paragraph roughly the same length. Of greater importance, however, is the need to balance the contents of each entry, using the same order of emphasis in each, preferably using a key sentence or phrase at the beginning.

The longer the paragraph, the more important it is to use a summary or conclusion with each. This style of list benefits from the use of subheads that summarize the contents of each entry with a word or phrase placed at the beginning.

The bullets used in a paragraph list replace paragraph indentations. Do not use indentations and bullets in combination. In order to heighten the visual distinction

---

Paragraphs with sub-heads on the same line:

- **Communicate effectively**. Team leaders must lead the movement to incorporate new procedures with written or verbal direction. This communication is critical to success and must be implemented throughout the division.

- **Empower action**. Team members who are effective at implementing new procedures must be recognized and rewarded. A performance management system is a critical component in producing this action.

- **Follow through**. New procedures may be implemented but have a short life unless they are supported. Both existing team members and new hires must understand the nature and purpose of new procedures in order to maintain momentum.

Paragraphs with sub-heads on a separate line:

- **Communicate effectively.**
  Team leaders must lead the movement to incorporate new procedures with written or verbal direction. This communication is critical to success and must be implemented throughout the division.

- **Empower action.**
  Team members who are effective at implementing new procedures must be recognized and rewarded. A performance management system is a critical component in producing this action.

- **Follow through.**
  New procedures may be implemented but have a short life unless they are supported. Both existing team members and new hires must understand the nature and purpose of new procedures in order to maintain momentum.

between entries, add a little extra space between entries (use about half the spacing of a full line, or 0.5" for 11 or 12 point text) and between the list and the rest of the text.

List Pairs

Two or more bulleted lists can be grouped together to emphasize differences, compare key points, or highlight contrasting information.

Such lists can be run side by side or one after the other. This application is also an effective way to reduce the overall size of a single list.

Pair options:

Pros/Cons	Increases/Decreases
Most/Least	First/Last
Cause/Effect	Problems/Solutions
Winners/Losers	Major/Minor
Old/New	Primary/Secondary
Close/Remote	General/Specific

List pairs work most effectively if they are placed close together. If the space is available to do so, run them side by side, or one directly after the other on the same page or slide. Design elements such as rules and frames can also be used to highlight the intended grouping.

A ranked set of items (organized from most to least) provides several options for producing a paired list. The easiest solution is to target only the highest-ranking numbers, for one list, moving the lowest-ranking numbers to another. Listing ranked items is typically done with numbered lists – 1., 2., 3., etc. – but when the list has a small number of entries, five or six at most, the ranking is still evident provided there is a consistent form.

In the same document, always follow the same form you begin with throughout the document, biggest on top, for example, as this provides a significant visual logic necessary to prevent confusion.

If you don't use numerals in a list, however, the obvious ranking may not be apparent unless there is additional

List pair samples:

Biggest changes in grocery sales:

INCREASES	DECREASES
• meal starters	frozen yogurt
• breakfast bars	frozen desert toppings
• butter	frozen orange juice

State growth in disposable personal income:

HIGHEST

- Nevada   +107 percent
- Utah   +90 percent
- Arizona   +87 percent

LOWEST

- D.C.   +34 percent
- Rhode Island +38 percent
- Alaska   +40 percent

Factors influencing growth:

Internal	External
• productivity	• economy
• employee training	• legislation
• research/development	• demographics
• technology upgrades	
• warehouse logistics	

information that would indicate one unit 'outranks' another. If some ranked entries have the same unit of measurement —two items are of equal value —it can be misleading to present one above the other unless there is additional information to provide the audience with the logic clues it needs to recognize this situation.

If you use two parallel lists to emphasize the top and bottom of a ranked order, be aware that an odd logic is at work. To be consistent, the top five in a list will have the same top-to-bottom ranking as the lowest five. Yet this means that the bottom five have a reversed order compared to the top five.

For example, in a total group of 15 items, the first item in the 'top five' category represents the number one largest quantity in the whole list. But in the 'bottom five' category, there is also a number one item, in this case presented the lowest quantity, or number 15 overall. To produce the top five list, you just select the top five entries, in order. To create the bottom five, you do the same, but work up from the bottom, 15, 14, 13, 12, etc.

Numbered Lists

Numbered entries are not only practical but necessary for some kinds of material. Yet they can also be distracting or misleading if used inappropriately.

In these lists, numbers replace bullets; **the two elements should not be used together.** If numbering is used, follow the same general guidelines for line length and spacing as with bullets to improve readability.

A numbered list is particularly helpful with complex outlines, lengthy document structures, or where there is a very long list of list entries. There is no hard and fast rule about when to use numbers and when not to, but logic and common sense can be a guide. Numbered lists and bulleted lists can also be used together present complex or lengthy contents.

Use numbers when the introduction or heading suggests, as in "Top Five Divisions" or "Six Functions of Good Management." Don't use numbered lists if the contents are not meant to represent a sequence or specific group.

The human brain is capable of recognizing small numbers or objects without numbering. If there are only three to five items for a list, the total number is obvious and numbering may be superfluous.

Most investment activity for shopping centers:

1. Grocery-anchored strip malls
2. Mixed-use facilities
3. Big box retailers/power centers
4. Main streets/urban centers
5. Lifestyle centers

Numbers and bullets can be combined to manage complex or lengthy material.

Conflict Management Process

1. **Analyze**
   - identify internal interests
   - identify opposition interests
   - diagnose with multiple perspectives

2. **Plan for negotiation**
   - identify standards and criteria to be used
   - list prioritized interests
   - develop alternatives
   - anticipate conflicts and conflict options

3. **Negotiate**
   - implement standards and criteria
   - explain specific internal interests
   - listen to specific opposition interests
   - jointly develop possible solutions

Logic Lists

A logic list can be used to summarize a complex progression of thought, to build an argument for a key point, or to follow a chain of events or facts that lead to a conclusion.

Using any of the traditional journalistic queries — Who, What, Where, When, and How (or Why) — this kind of bulleted list can provide a quick supporting structure that adds argumentative value to content. The title or lead-in line is a critical part of this format, used as an explanatory introduction with key concepts or elements providing the reader with an appropriate clue as to what is going on in the list that follows.

A sequence of stages or steps provides one type of logic list option.

Project management steps:
- Select key members.
- Designate assignments.
- Provide adequate support.
- Benchmark progress.
- Evaluate results.
- Reward achievements.

A series of questions can be presented in list form as an organizational structure or guide.

Key questions for information designers:
- Are readers able to find information?
- Can readers understand the information?
- How do readers respond to the information?

Questions are valid content in this kind of list. A question can be used as a lead-in and the contents provide answers or options. Or, the list itself can be a series of questions, a useful strategy for presentations and group sessions.

Paired lists also have great advantages when dealing with logical presentations. Displayed in tandem, such duos simplify and emphasize tightly linked concepts such as pros and cons, external and internal factors, supply and demand, and similar categories.

Bulleted lists provide a structured format to present logic sequences, such as those used in business plans and revenue models.

Revenue Assumptions

- Average price per unit $11.00
- Unit sales volume   27,000
- Fee per unit   3.5 percent
- Revenue per unit $0.39
- Gross sales revenue $297,000
- *Total revenue from fees*   *$10,395*

List Strategy

- *The style of bullets and lists can be objective, persuasive, or personal.*

Bulleted material plays a key role in communications. The use of bullets is an effective tactic when presenting and organizing information intended to persuade, compare, describe, or summarize. The facts and supporting material that are key in this action can be segregated, organized, and highlighted with bulleted lists, delivering them more efficiently to its intended audience.

Key strategies for bulleted lists:

- Reduce the amount of time necessary to exchange information.
- Emphasize major points.
- Organize and present increments of logic and support for arguments,
- Provide a visual break from the monotony of longer sections of text.
- Reduce ambiguity.

Any or all of these strategies are accomplished in part by generating lists in place of longer blocks of text or combining it with text, charts, or graphs. And the impact is increased when the writing style is appropriate for the material and the audience.

In general, business writing is impersonal. Similar to the style used in academic publications, personalized elements are avoided in favor of this kind of objective approach. But variations on this theme are common, with individual companies and organizations following their own internal models.

Information Targets

Three general types of information are used in written business communications. The impact of each changes according to the level of authority attached to the person reading it.

- text (words)
- word pictures (lists, matrices, charts)
- images (photos, graphs, drawings, symbols)

Typically, executives have less time to read and lists or images have higher impact. Lower down the corporate structure, staff members and managers have more time to read and words have a higher impact.

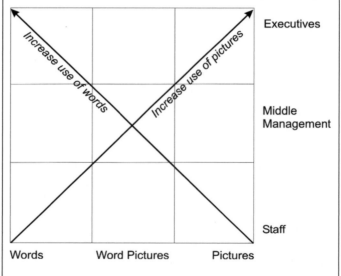

Developed by The Executive Leadership Group (Denver, CO) www.ExecutiveLeadershipGroup.com. Used with permission.

Personalized writing is found more often in advertising and marketing situations than elsewhere, and for good reason. Research has shown it is an effective tool, generating positive responses from most readers, even when used in some technical applications. But if used out of place, it can also produce a disconcerting, unwelcome effect in readers, diminishing or negating the intended impact of the text.

The goal of business writing is to communicate, but this can be done with active or passive verbs, objective or subjective approaches, and personal or impersonal style. Successful writing is not so much about picking the right style as matching the right style to the audience.

One communication style used within some organizations relates to the use of "shared values." Here, personalized pronouns such as "we" and "our" are employed to establish and emphasize collective membership in the organization, corporation, or activity. If this style is already in place, it may be the preferred — or even mandated — style, requiring writers to follow its conventions. Otherwise, the impersonal form takes precedence.

Personal form:	Our quarterly goals.
	We anticipate ...
Impersonal form:	The quarterly goals.
	It is anticipated ...

Adjectives are a key part of business writing style and do not have to be avoided in lists. In general, however, they should be selected and evaluated based on objective use, clarifying and defining rather than exaggerating or glorifying.

Adjectives are a key component for persuasive writing — text created to support or argue for a position — but not all text should be persuasive. In some kinds of reports, the goal is to present information impartially, with the

Who's the Audience?

Business style depends as much on its intended audience as its designated purpose. Executives do not read full-sized business documents and often not even paragraphs within executive summaries. Staff members, however, typically require full access to details and descriptions, relying on this content to write summaries and condensations for those higher up the totem pole.

For all levels of academic and corporate structure, the writer's ability to tailor a document or list style to the audience is directly linked to the success of the writing. Knowledge of the audience includes identifying existing style sheets and guidelines, rules that apply to documents and presentations, and recognizing established cultural and stylistic conventions.

AUDIENCE	EFFECTIVE ATTENTION SPAN
Top level, executive.	shortest
Mid-level, management.	
Low-level, functionary.	longest

reader making an objective decision based on the quality of the information and the facts it represents. Here, adjectives may signal a lack of impartiality, which harms the communication goals of the material.

Busy executives typically depend on facts and will generate their own conclusions from evaluation rather than persuasion. Researchers, managers, or lower level workers, on the other hand, may react more positively to active persuasion, even though objectivity is still expected.

Research on how online users react to information on Web pages reinforces the need for writers to work carefully with adjectives. In this media environment, most users report a preference for objective, non-persuasive prose. This is especially true of list contents, as this format is widely used on Web sites and is an efficient means of organizing and presenting information.

Persuasive adjectives include such modifiers as "wonderful," "exciting," and "revolutionary"; evaluative adjectives are less subjective and more comparative, words such as "biggest," "newest," and "most efficient." Informative adjectives are also evaluative, modifying key words with more descriptive terms such as "green," "cube-shaped," or "locally-made."

In print documents and slide presentations, the impact of lists is improved with the same attention to informative writing style. The choice of active verbs rather than passive ones, however, can help make this kind of writing more direct and effective.

No matter the target audience or the format for a bulleted list, your first goal should always be the same: **make your point clearly and do it early.** Business writing — and lists in particular — is not an appropriate place to hide information or keep audiences guessing.

Target Audience

- *The style of a list should relate directly to its intended audience.*

As with all forms of business and academic communication, the writer achieves greater success by identifying and adopting style conventions based on the intended audience. Before business writing can be made truly effective, the contents must be matched to the audience.

Executives and other decision makers have been shown to dislike text with personalized, persuasive, or evaluative styles. Effective presentations made for this audience are typically shorter, contain more summarized material, and make greater use of bulleted lists because executives have less time to become informed, relying on shorter writing formats to deliver highlights and key points rather than details.

In this context, the decision-making process depends more on facts and reliable information and less on personal alliances. This reaction is not only found at the top; most business professionals prefer information text to that which is persuasive or evaluative. In business reading, the goal is to gain information and in this context, the goal may be impeded by the use of style which seems inappropriate to the audience.

Most readers of business documents read them in a linear fashion, from beginning to end. This doesn't mean that they read every word, or even every section, but the flow of communication is closely related to the structure of the document being read. Thus, introductions and conclusions can both be important elements, but neither necessarily replaces the "meat" in the middle.

In some layers of corporate bureaucracy, the longest reports are read by those lowest in the organization, with rewritten summaries generated for those in higher positions. The original material may still be critical, but it shrinks on its way to the top.

Executives and decision makers are more likely to scan documents, picking out only information that is pertinent or conclusive. Especially when such leaders read longer documents, they focus and skip based on what they need to know. In this environment, headlines, summaries, and bulleted lists are an asset to the flow of information, even if they do not replace longer text passages.

Bulleted lists have a useful function in almost all kinds of business documents and presentations, but they vary in importance based on the audience. In general, the higher the level of management or decision making, the shorter the document and the more critical the list. But even the longest, most detailed report benefits from concise writing and careful placement of conclusions, summaries, and key concepts.

Audience Characteristics

Companies and organizations often have existing sets of guidelines and standards applying to writing for internal use. These can supercede any strategies or goals that a writer may have. Otherwise, the following factors are influential in determining what a person reads, and why, and are important elements to consider.

- age
- professional status
- available time
- gender
- socio/economic background
- level of education
- status/level of authority
- work experience
- primary language

Creating a List

- *Concepts, facts, and conclusions ideal for list use can be discovered and extracted from existing material.*

List contents can be created from scratch or extracted and condensed from existing material. The first step is to identify the ideas that can or should be converted to list form. Use journalistic queries in this process, the standard questions, Who, What, Where, When, Why, and How?

Conclusions, summaries, or highlights already exist in most business text, often at the beginnings and ends of documents. Not surprisingly, this includes sections entitled "introduction," "discussion," "conclusions," and "summary."

The most obvious candidate for listing is any text that already uses a number or quantity to introduce multiple items. Scan sentences for usage such as: "The following three factors ...," "Seven major steps ...," or "Multiple phases in this process include ..."

When such preliminary markers are not available, scan for series of items within paragraphs, looking for words or phrases separated by commas or semi-colons. Repetition by pattern or series also points out listable elements, including proper nouns, labels, titles, or other similar material.

Key words and phrases that emphasize major points are typically grouped at the beginning and end of sections or paragraphs. And an opening or closing paragraph in a chapter or section is more likely than others to introduce or sum up major points; the same is true for leading and ending sentences within paragraphs.

Complex sentences with multiple key points are an obvious target for reformating in lists. These can be converted by extracting key points and rewriting in a shorter,

Original sentence:

Benefits range from productivity gains and reduction of working capital to an increase in customer satisfaction.

Bulleted version:

Benefits:
- increased productivity
- reduced working capital
- increased customer satisfaction

Original paragraph:

The quest for greater market share is behind many investment decisions for e-business. But the future of commerce online also promises reduced costs, increased efficiency, and greater customer retention. Concerns about return on investment are also met, as spending in this form of technology is expected to pay for itself.

Bulleted version:

E-business investment factors:
- greater market share
- reduced costs
- increased efficiency
- increased customer retention
- improved return on investment

condensed form. Phrases that indicate new and/or key information are often found as clauses introduced by the familiar words "that" and "which."

List targets include: nouns, proper names, key words, facts, statistics, measurements, actions, divisions, time frames, movement, change factors, comparisons, indicators, metrics, goals, processes, ideas, strategies, tactics, phases, and assessments. But any element of text or thought that can be divided in unique segments is potential material in this quest.

For effective list production, consider the initial production to be only the first step. Produce whatever is thought necessary or critical, following a consistent program of condensation, simplification, and excerption. Then, once an initial "beta list" has been developed, use additional steps to modify the list for optimum length.

For existing text, lists can be generated with four different processes — **simplification**, **condensation**, and **extraction**.

- **Simplification** Text is reduced in length by deleting words and replacing complex phrases or sentences with shorter, more concise versions. Simplification can be used to reduce wordiness and make complex ideas more understandable.

- **Condensation** Longer runs of text are replaced with digested text that summarizes key points. A condensation focuses only on key points, combining ideas or phrases into shorter statements, often skipping intermediate points. Typically, a condensation will reduce original material by a target amount, half or one third, for example. An abstract or summary is a form of condensation, representing the complete content of a document or document section. An executive summary is an example of an abstract, as is a conclusion.

- **Extraction**   A single word, statistic, fact, phrase, quotation, sentence, or short passage is removed untouched from its surrounding text. Such activity can be used to reinforce and emphasize because removed from surrounding text, the shorter length of items in a bulleted list gives them added significance. This kind of list application can be done parallel to the text — leaving the original material intact, with the list item repeating the original — or as a stand-alone element.

List-Writing Style

- *Lists are short and concise in order to attract attention and impart information. All elements of list style should enhance these factors.*

The list is used as an informative device, attracting attention and presenting contents in short, condensed chunks. To make this device achieve its effect, the text must be written to match the contents, projecting information without wasting space or diluting the facts. Sparse, informative writing is the method of choice to accomplish this goal.

Simpler = shorter. Just as in standard text, items in a list suffer from bloating. Unneeded or repetitive words or phrases not only obscure the intent of an item, but the extra length involved has an unwanted effect on the main object of a list, to attract the reader's eye with shorter line length than other text.

- *Make your point.* Put the most important terms or conclusions first. Key points should be the first entries in lists and the first terms in entries.

- *Develop and maintain parallel construction.* The same placement and use of nouns, verbs, and modifiers should be applied for each entry. All entries should begin with a noun, for example, or all begin with a verb, but not a combination of the two in the same list.

This:
- Acknowledge input
- Explain group interests
- Implement standards

Not this:
- Acknowledge input
- Explain group interests
- Standards are necessary

What's the Point?

Most business writing suffers from a single major flaw: readers have to do too much work to get the point. Bulleted lists, being condensed forms of business writing, often suffer from the same malady. When writing or revising any business writing, the single most effective tactic for effective communications: **put conclusions, summaries, and key facts first**.

Where to make your point:

- First section in a document.

- First paragraph in a section.

- First sentence in a paragraph.

- First entry in a list.

- First point in a sentence or phrase.

- *Balance related key words.* Parallel construction is a must in lists, with nouns, verbs, and modifiers following a consistent style and placement. Individual entries as well as all entries in a list should be organized in a logical structure that readers will grasp as common sense.

  This way:
  Benefits to small, medium, and large-sized companies.

  Not this way:
  Both small and medium-sized companies, as well as larger enterprises, will gain benefits.

Hit List

Vague, over-used, and wordy phrases and expressions should be targeted for removal. Some examples:

    it can be considered ... it is understood that ...
    it is my understanding ...   on the basis of ...
    we refer to ...   with reference to ...
    research indicates that ... as a general rule ...

Other targets for deletion include:

as noted	the extent of
in general	the fact that
in reality	the field of
in size	the idea of
in the amount of	the issue of
in the form of	the level of
in the realm of	the magnitude of
in the space of	the month of
in the way of	the nature of
in this area	the presence of
involved in	the problem of
is (are) known as	the process of
made of	the result of
of all	the state of
one of	there is
particular	this particular
respective	to the extent
the act of	under the circumstances
the basis of	very
the business of	which is (are)
the city of	who is (are)
the concept of	years old

- *Use strong verbs.* Target weak and passive verbs for replacement. Weak verbs are the most commonly used variety and in passive form are often found in combination with other words. Examples include: is, are, has, have, do, does, etc. Active alternatives are preferred because they convey a stronger image in less space. Replace verb phrases — to come to, to reach a conclusion — with single verbs — come, conclude. Replace gerunds (verbs with -ing that are used as nouns) and similar nouns with active verb forms.

  This:
  Management controls production.

  Not this:
  Management has control over production.

  This:
  The Romans defeated the Huns.

  Not this:
  The Romans were victorious over the Huns.

  This:
  Profits are maintained.

  Not this:
  Maintaining profits.

- *Use passive verbs to stress* what *rather than* how. In some cases, passive verbs are preferred because they emphasize what is happening.

  This:
  Employee retention was improved by human resources initiatives.

  Not this:
  Human resources initiatives improved employee retention.

- *Use gerunds to replace phrases.* Passive words such as gerunds should not be avoided altogether. In some cases, they are an effective method to shorten longer passages.

  This:
  The development of new products.

  Becomes:
  Developing new products.

- *Avoid the past tense.* Unless the context requires it, use another verb form instead.

- *Drop verbs.* Verb usage such as "to change" or "to have success" provides an opportunity to drop one or more words. In some lists, verbs can be dropped completely. Rewrite, change word order, or use a dash (—) or colon (:) as a shortcut for a verb or verb phrase in an entry to reduce line length.

  This:
  Gross sales were $150 million.

  Becomes:
  Gross sales: $150 million.

  Or: $150 million gross sales.

  This:
  Technology has added return on investment.

  Becomes:
  Technology adds return on investment.

  This:
  Adopt global data standards for products, communications, and transactions.

Becomes:
Global data standards for products, communications, and transactions.

This:
Evaluation techniques focus on decreasing human errors.

Becomes:
Evaluation techniques to decrease human errors.

- *Reduce the number of words used to create meaning.* The placement of words in some sentences and phrases can be shifted, allowing prepositions and other supporting terms to be dropped.

    This:
    Reduction in investment cost.

    Becomes:
    Reduced investment.

    This:
    Making payments on time.

    Becomes:
    On-time payments.

    This:
    The programming of software.

    Becomes:
    Software programming.

- *Replace cumbersome expressions with shorter alternatives.* Simplifying text reduces complexity, which improves readability. Exceptions include technical terminology that is accepted practice within an organization.

This:
minimize.

Not this:
reduce to a minimum.

This:
old

Not this:
advanced in years.

- *Avoid redundancy.* Many common expressions contain repetitive or redundant concepts. Replace or rewrite to say what you mean in a shorter form.

  This:
  current status

  Becomes:
  status

  This:
  advance plan

  Becomes:
  plan

  This:
  The state of Massachusetts

  Becomes:
  Massachusetts

- *Drop the small words.* In regular text, common prepositions, articles, and conjunctions — a, an, the, of, and, etc. — combine to produce about one third of all words used. In the shorter, concise environment of lists, many of these short terms can be omitted. Adjectives such as *our* are also apt targets if the context makes them superfluous.

This:
The profits from product extensions.

Becomes:
Profits from product extensions.

- *Drop the use of "that."* This common word is used frequently in sentences as a conjunction or pronoun but is often unnecessary, especially in list entries. Which, often incorrectly used in place of that (correctly used, that introduces restrictive clauses and which is used with nonrestrictive clauses) is also open for removal.

This:
Divisions that outsource hiring are profitable.

Becomes:
Profitable divisions outsource hiring.

- *Begin entries with subjects instead of prepositions.* Rearrange the elements of a sentence or phrase, beginning with the subject. The result is a stronger, more active statement and fewer words.

This:
In 2002, it was Team A leading in innovation.

Becomes:
Team A led in innovation in 2002.

This:
There are 17 divisions in each section.

Becomes:
17 divisions in each section.

- *Use concrete modifiers.* Replace vague or ill-defined quantities or measurement with more specific qualifiers or comparisons. Vague qualifiers include: about, a

Replace List

Replace ...	With ...
a large segment of	many
as a general rule	generally
at this time	now
at all times	always
close proximity	close
conduct an examination	examine
continues on	continues
contractual agreement	contract
current status	status
final outcome	outcome
give consideration	consider
in order to	to
in the absence of	without
in the neighborhood	about
in the vicinity	near
majority of the time	usually
on a continuing basis	continually
over the long term	ultimately
perform analysis of	analyze
plan of attack	plan
place emphasis on	emphasize
take action	act
together with	with
ultimate outcome	outcome
until the time when	until
whether or not	whether
with the exception of	except

number of, better, big, few, large, many, near, several, small, some.

This:
Increased sales.

Or:
Sales increase of 25 percent.

Not this:
Better sales.

This:
50,000 sq. foot production space.

Not this:
Large production facilities.

- *Use nouns or names instead of pronouns to refer to specific things.* Lists and list entries are often noticed and read independently of their context, requiring list content to be specific as much as possible to avoid being vague or ambiguous.

  This:
  Diagnose Team A's performance.

  Not this:
  Diagnose its performance.

- *Split multiple elements into separate items.* A major goal of bulleted lists is the creation of a short emphatic steps, a kind of prose poem that provides a visual alternative to the longer style of regular prose. This goal is best accomplished if each entry is restricted to a single concept.

This:
- planning
- support
- analysis

Not this:
- planning, support, and analysis

- *Organize to reduce the use of repetitive words.* Lists are an ideal platform for emphasis, which can be enhanced by moving repetitive words to the lead-in line or title.

  This:
  Enhanced message content includes:
  - Repetition
  - Structure
  - Readability

  Not this:
  Enhanced content includes:
  - Message repetition
  - Message structure
  - Message readability

- *Replace spelled-out numbers with numerals.* This convention saves space, but in some cases it may be counter-productive. Spelled-out numbers are scanned and comprehended quicker than numerals, helping maintain the flow of reading, a useful characteristic in some list applications.

  This:
  Seventeen field offices.

  Becomes:
  17 field offices.

- *Use themes or shared characteristics to replace multiple items.*

   This:
   Buses, light rail, and subways.

   Becomes:
   Public transportation.

   This:
   Activities designed to discover, test, and demonstrate results.

   Becomes:
   Experiments.

- *Combine related words.* Using a forward slash (/) or hyphen (-), related terms can be linked to save space. This is a delicate decision, however, as the result must be instantly recognizable to its audience, make sense, and not reduce the intended impact of either word.

This:	Becomes:
costs and benefits	costs/benefits
profit and loss	profit/loss
strategy and tactics	strategy/tactics

- *Rephrase descriptive clauses.* Clauses that describe people or things can be rewritten, cutting the number of words while emphasizing the descriptive factor.

   This:
   Donald Brown, who is the president of Acme Consulting.

   Becomes:
   Donald Brown, president of Acme Consulting

   Or this:
   Acme Consulting President Donald Brown

- *Use sentence or phrase structure to emphasize.* Word arrangement can work to obscure or emphasize key points. The latter is the objective in lists.

  This:
  Teenagers spent $170 billion in 2002.

  Becomes:
  Teen spending in 2002: $170 billion.

- *Use bold or italics to emphasize key information.* Emphasis can be added within lists with the use of bold or italic type. Avoid using capital letters — especially all caps — or underlining to achieve this effect, as these can look tacky and unprofessional.

  This:
  Diagnose **conflict**.

  Not this:
  Diagnose CONFLICT.

Concise Lists and Entries

- *Short lists and short list entries are preferable to long lists and long list entries.*

Most of the time, you can't beat short as the most efficient way to gain attention and impart comprehension in business writing. The same holds true for bulleted lists. The fewer words in a list item, the more it stands out from other text and the more likely it is to be read by its intended audience. This is the key factor behind the most effective bulleted lists. And it's backed up by research.

Eye span refers to the amount of text the human eye focuses on during short stops, or fixations, that occur during in reading activity. In most people, this averages about 30 characters, the width of one to three standard words. If a bulleted list entry is short enough, the eye can span it with one fixation, improving the potential of rapid communication.

Don't confuse short length with less time writing, however. Often, it takes more time to condense a chunk of text or an idea than it does to write it in the first place.

Condensing is a process combining craft and art. The craft part is the selection of appropriate words and placement, using existing rules of grammar, syntax, and spelling. The writer's art applies beyond these rules, turning concept into communication. Both craft and art are required to produce the short, concise content needed in lists.

Unfortunately, lists do not exist in a vacuum; they represent facts and concepts representing the authority and strategies of executives, managers, departments, or organizations. Even though short, concise lists might benefit everyone, existing guidelines and office politics may dictate what and how much must be written.

RULE OF THUMB
List Length

- general rule: 3 to 6 entries per list
- slide presentations — 1 list per slide
- Web pages — 1 list per screen
- printed documents — 1 list per page page

Content itself can determine length despite the need to limit list length. Technical information, statistics, legal content, and other material may require longer structures for accuracy, also overruling list limitations.

What is the optimum length for a list? For screen presentations — on computer monitors, laptop displays, or projected displays — three to six entries represent an ideal range. This has nothing to do with the intent of the presenter or the amount of original material. It is based on visual logic and what audiences have come to expect in the rapidly-expanding environment of list usage. One slide holds one list, and if the list is too long, audience interest strays.

The same is even more important for Web pages, where scrolling is a critical issue. List lengths here should be confined to the average screen size, both vertically and horizontally, allowing users to see the entire list without the need to shift positions.

In printed documents, page breaks create a practical limiter for list lengths. With this traditional format the contents should be edited, altered, or shifted in position to keep a list unbroken on a page. Other text formats are also typically mixed with lists in a printed document, placing further pressure on lists to be short and concise for the best visual contrast.

List-Shortening Tactics

- *It's easier to find material to put in a list than to decide what to take out.*

Often, the collection of material for a list is too successful, leading to a list that is overly long. The task then turns to editing for length, a process that focuses on the identification of excess entries and those that are too wordy.

Editing for length has more in common with Attila the Hun than St. Francis of Assissi. It often requires brutal decisions, ripping out cherished material, excising clever adjectives and adverbs, and the application of other ego-deflating tools without undermining the value of the original information.

List length editing follows many of the same principles as generating list copy in the first place. Most of the work involves cutting, combining, and condensing. Design decisions, however, are also useful here, reducing line lengths with larger margins, for example, rather than deleting them, or dividing one long list into two.

List Shortening: Step One

- Identify and remove repetitive words, unnecessary adjectives, and weak or flawed supporting phrases. Often, shorter forms of the same phrase can be substituted and the result is not only a shorter line length, but crisper, clearer text. For example, replace "Sharing of information" with "Information sharing" or drop "Strategic goals that are unsupported" in favor of "Unsupported strategic goals."

List Shortening: Step Two

• Rank list items in order of intended emphasis, importance, or any other appropriate logic. This ranking generates a platform with which to spot weak or inconsistent elements, repetition, and out-of-place items, each a potential target for removal. With a ranking in place, the list can also be scanned for an appropriate threshold, a practical cut-off point beyond which entries can be cut.

List Shortening: Step Three

• A list that is too long may provide ample opportunity for a split into two or more sub-lists. Appropriate targets for pairing: most and least, pros and cons, highs and lows, and befores and afters. See *List Pairs* for more potential targets. Use the Who, What, Where, When, Why, and How questions to identify similarities or themes in this application. In any of these cases, the number of split elements may not balance, but as long as there are at least two or three elements per list, this strategy works.

List Shortening: Step Four

• If you are using PowerPoint or another slide presentation program, a single bulleted list can be presented in sequence rather than as a whole. Here, each additional entry is added to the original slide one line at a time during the presentation, diminishing the negative effects of a longer initial list.

Crediting Sources

- *The short, concise information presented in lists gains validity when proper sources are credited.*

The believability of list contents is improved when it is linked to appropriate sources. Particularly in business use, lists are objective resources and their contents influence additional use. This focuses responsibility on the writer to properly acknowledge the source of facts, statistics, conclusions, and other principal material.

Copyrighted material in regular text can be set in italic, bold, within quote marks, or set apart with different margins than the surrounding text in order to signify its uniqueness. With no limitations on space in this format, sources and credits are also easily managed, by inserting names directly with the material used, in brackets nearby, or in footnotes.

But bulleted lists rarely offer the luxury of adequate space. This short-text format could lose impact if unnecessarily stretched out with the details of its sources. But whether using regular text or bulleted lists, the rules and traditions of copyright use and fair attribution must be followed, for legal if not ethical reasons.

Number of self-employed workers in 2000:
- 3.2 million   managerial/professional specialties
- 2.1 million   technical, sales, administrative support
- 1.2 million   service occupations
- 3.5 million   other

Source: U.S. Bureau of Labor Statistics

One solution is to use smaller type when citing sources, or set them to the side or at the bottom of a list or slide. If it is necessary to cite a source for each item in a list, this information can be displayed in smaller type next to each entry. Footnote marks can also be used, with the footnote text presented at the end of the list. Unless publishing guidelines require footnotes and sources to be grouped at the end of a document, they provide quicker, more useful attribution placed at the point of use.

A general rule of thumb for downsizing copyright and source material in printed documents is to make it 2 to 4 points smaller than the type used in the list itself. That is, if a list is set in 11 point type, the credits would be displayed at 7 to 9 points. The same general contrast works with slide presentations and Web pages, but space and appearance issues may require more dramatic reductions.

To maintain the short-format appeal of the list, shorten the credit material as much as possible. In the list environment, it is unnecessary to use complete sentences, or even phrases, just the fewest number of words needed to generate an appropriate label.

This:
The statistics used here came from the Bureau of Labor Statistics.

Becomes:
Bureau of Labor Statistics

Or: BLS

List credits used in executive summaries, memos, presentations, and other short documents do not require all of the information traditionally used to cite sources. At minimum, a publication name and date may be acceptable. Use one or two of these facts in a short-form source citation:

- magazine or journal   • article title   • book title
- author   • organization or business name
- year, month if available

Bullet Proofing

- *In the short, concise environment of lists,
  mistakes have nowhere to hide.*

Bulleted lists are used to attract attention and present condensed information. This practical use comes at a price. Focused attention also focuses fault-finding and criticism. Typos, misspellings, and other errors that may be hidden in the text of a long paragraph stand out in sharp detail in the sparse surroundings of a list.

List writers take on a special burden because of this side effect. They must take special care to avoid mistakes, care that is best employed during the research and writing itself. But no matter the care with which lists are constructed in the first place, the work is not done until the final material has been double-checked for errors.

Proofing lists includes spelling, grammar, punctuation, continuity, and other elements covered in this book. Areas requiring special attention are those involved with summaries, condensations, or other rewriting of existing material. Here, the effort to shorten can easily produce errors of omission or misstatements of fact.

Ask these pertinent questions as part of the proofing process:

- Is this what was meant in the original?
- Did I leave out something that was important in the original statement?
- Did I include something that was not in the original statement?

The final action in proofing — too often missing in critical documents, lists, and business documents in general — is fact checking. A fact can be any unit of information, including names, places, dates, measurements,

List Proofing Checklist

❏ spelling	❏ parallel construction
❏ verb tense	❏ word placement (syntax)
❏ redundancy	❏ unnecessary words/phrases
❏ capitalization	❏ punctuation
❏ margins	❏ type style
❏ line spacing	❏ bullet style
❏ bullet size	❏ bullet spacing
❏ alignment	❏ credits
❏ grammar	

and statistics. Because of the high probability of being noticed, the simplest facts are the most liable to be recognized by the most people. Unfortunately, these are also the most likely to be skipped over during proofing.

Details, measurements, statistics, and other nuggets of information may not be recognized by anyone but the writer, yet these are appropriate elements for accuracy because the audience trusts they are correct.

Key elements that carry the most dangerous bite, however, are not standard facts but personal or localized information. Is it the Oakland Museum, or the Oakland Museum of California? Is your employer's name spelled Elliot or Elliott? Get one of these wrong, especially in front of a home audience, and your credibility suffers, perhaps permanently.

Proofing of these standard and personal details is called fact checking and it can be more diabolical to perform than other editing chores. Not only do individual facts easily slip through the proofing process without alerting attention, but the condensation process often involved with list-making can introduce omissions, misstatements, or other errors. Fact checking involves comparing written material to original sources, double-checking critical elements, and generally being paranoid about everything.

Fact checking require access to reliable sources for correct spelling and usage. Business directories, almanacs, trade publications, online resources, and libraries are appropriate tools for this process, but it may also revert to a simpler technique: calling the source involved and asking.

Prime fact-checking categories:

- company name
- executive name
- any person's name
- title, rank, occupation, professional credentials
- state, city, or county of location
- year or other detail of date
- accomplishment, activity, or performance
- ownership, creative source, or vested interest

RULE OF THUMB
Bullet Proofing

- Check every fact as if it will be read by someone directly connected to the fact itself.
- If it's too obvious to check, it's the most likely to be wrong.
- The closer to home, the more embarrassing the error.
- The shorter the list, the more glaring the error.

The Rule of Consistency

- *Consistency is not noticed unless it is missing.*

You may think that consistency is just one more rule that grammarians and micro-managing editors have invented to suit their own nit-picking sense of order in an already over-controlling universe. Not so.

Consistency provides a powerful but invisible boost to effective communications. When information if presented in a consistent style and format, it has a better chance for comprehension by readers because they do not have to wrestle with apparently arbitrary elements. Consistency is a powerful force because it reduces ambiguity.

If one item in a list, for example, uses a different style, organization, or format than all the other elements, that item is emphasized — consciously or unconsciously — in the eye of the reader. Such inconsistent elements create friction and barriers to the seamless scanning of content, slowing down the pace of reading and diminishing the intended meaning.

The act of writing, editing, and design can be refined to develop and maintain consistency. But any craft developed or honed here is not as important as the most important tool: proofreading. There's no magic formulae or great skill required for this task, just tedious checking.

With bullets and lists, an additional application of consistency is required. The first is **local** — each list must be consistent within itself — and the other **global** — the same elements must be consistent throughout the document or presentation.

Using Jargon

- *The key words of an industry or profession are essential for effective communication, but when out-of-place or overused, have a negative effect.*

The inside language of a business, industry, or profession can provide an effective communications shortcut. Shared knowledge of key words, phrases, and other unique language permits insiders to comprehend information quickly.

This vocabulary, sometimes called "jargon," is a form of communication that dominates the military, the computer industry, and the medical profession, and it is often an expected standard. Unfortunately, jargon can also hamper communications. Someone who is not familiar with insider language does not benefit from its use; they are confused because the meaning is unknown or unclear. And even in context and among peers, jargon can be very effective at putting an audience to sleep.

Jargon includes buzz words, acronyms, euphemisms, shop talk, and insider slang. Among these, buzz words may be the most deceptive. Typically newly-coined, they impart freshness and a cutting edge spirit to business presentations, assuming both the user and the audience understand what they mean. The problem with buzz words is that no one can tell when or if they will pass over the invisible border from fresh to passé. And sooner or later, most buzz words lose their buzz.

The best guides for jargon use — and avoidance — are documents and presentations already in use within an organization or group. As with writing style, match the words with the audience. It is as much a mistake to present unfamiliar terms to an audience as it is to avoid known ones with another.

Corporations are more prone to jargon abuse than are specific industries or professions. Buzzwords in particular are a dangerous temptation for executives, managers, and consultants, often linked to hot new concepts or trends. The real problem with business buzzwords is not that they aren't useful, but that many of them are used inappropriately, too often, or too late.

Like much street slang, buzzwords come and go with great frequency. Anchored inside a document, they may quickly shift from a adding patina of freshness to imparting an odor of staleness.

Slang suffers a similar defect. On the street, it is the voice of change, the cutting-edge where language of the future is being created. In the office and general environment of business writing, however, slang is typically out of place, too casual for proper communication. As with buzz words, use with caution or not at all.

RULE OF THUMB
Jargon Justification

- Use acronyms or abbreviations only if they are standard usage for the intended audience.
- Add definitions for acronyms and abbreviations the first time they are used.
- Replace questionable terms with plain English equivalents.
- Dump nouns that end in -wise or -ation in favor of their shorter equivalents.
- Replace verbs that end in -ize with simpler forms.

Other Bullets

- *In some cases, a single bullet can be used with a statement in order to tag it with special emphasis.*

Even though a single item is a not a list, the use of a just one bullet performs the same function, emphasizing the material it accompanies.

The key factor in managing teams: • accountability.

Single bullet usage should follow the same design conventions for lists. Particularly important: if you use a bullet in this application, limit the use of other emphatic elements, including bold, italics, underlining, and all caps. Single bullets are also potentially disruptive to the visual order of a print document, Web page, or slide presentation. If used too often — more than once or twice a page — the effect is diminished by clutter.

Unconventional bullet use can also include listed or grouped items that are not arranged in a traditional vertical format. In this application, however, there is a thin margin between effectiveness and overuse.

Certified training in:
- Java   • Flash   • Visual Basic   • XML

When used in this kind of horizontal format, the bullets and the items they precede should be evenly spaced. Too much or too little space between entries produces visual confusion.

Another application for bullets is with nested lists, a list format where a second set of indents is added. A nested list is only one step away from an outline, and the former may be a more practical application depending on the amount of material and its complexity.

Numbered lists as well may be more appropriate formats whenever a bulleted list begins branching into this additional territory. The rule of thumb for nested lists and bullets is to use no more than one extra level. If additional nested structure is needed, use an outline format instead.

Layout and design features of nested lists should complement and extend the basic features of the main bulleted entries. Use the same type font, but variations in line spacing and type size are acceptable in order to make the two kinds of list elements distinctive.

The same bullet style is repeated for the secondary elements, but the size of the bullets should be reduced so that the secondary entries do not compete in emphasis with the primary entries. Other marks may also be substituted for the bullets used in the primary entries, such as a ■ bullet or a dash, either of which helps readers understand the intent of the organization.

With nested lists, use a combination of type sizes, line spacing, margins, or bullet sizes to produce visual distinction between primary and secondary entries.

Employment

- retail trade
  — general goods
  — food
  — apparel
  — eating/drinking
- services
  — lodging
  — legal
  — auto repair
  — health

Employment

- retail trade
  • general goods
  • food
  • apparel
  • eating/drinking
- services
  • lodging
  • legal
  • auto repair
  • health

Web Bullets

Web pages present significant challenges for bullet users. The overwhelming competition for attention in this expanding medium require Web designers to use the maximum amount of attention-grabbing devices, but Web pages that are too busy or cluttered may repel site visitors. Also, credibility of information on the Internet can be questionable because of the lack of editorial accountability at many sites, driving the need for design that reinforces a sense of objectivity.

In this environment, the use of bulleted lists works well, but unlike paper or slide projections, the computer screens on which Web pages are viewed provide relatively low resolution and most computer monitors are still well below the resolution of print.

Another difficulty: Web pages are constructed with the HTML (Hypertext markup language) standard, a programming language that includes a built-in bulleted list format, but this format limits fonts and layouts to preset options.

The two major Web browsers, Netscape and Microsoft Explorer, interpret HTML slightly differently and can alter the look of an original page design. Plus, users view Web pages on screens that have different dimensions and different viewing protocols, further varying the appearance of a given page.

All this narrows the choices for bulleted lists on the Web unless text is created in another format — such as Adobe Acrobat (pdf), which allows full control over type fonts and layouts — but the drawback is significantly longer times for pages to be downloaded.

Bulleted lists must conform to the lowest level of screen usage, not the highest, in order to ensure their maximum usefulness. Even though most of an audience may have the latest, high resolution models, there will always be some eyes staring at a presentation on an obsolete monitor that was manufactured years or decades earlier.

As for writing, most business text written for the Web benefits from an objective, impersonal style. Facts, logic, and plain prose perform best here amid hype and questionable content.

Guidelines for the use of bullets and list entries on Web pages:

- **Type selection.** Keep it simple, Times Roman or Georgia for serif; Arial or Tahoma for sans serif. Georgia and Tahoma were designed specifically for maximum readability on computer monitors.

- **Type size.** Keep text size at 12 to 14 points, using a smaller size if necessary for source information. Stick to the same size for all text used throughout an online presentation.

- **Type style.** Use normal type and avoid italics, bold, underlining, or all caps. The exception is headlines, subheads, or sparing use to emphasize key terms.

- **Line spacing**. For longer entries or lists of clickable links, add a little extra space between entries, but not as much as a full blank line.

- **Length**. List entries can run more than one line, but the complete width of the list must be visible in a single screen and the complete length of the list must also fit on a single screen. The optimum line length should not exceed four or five words.

- **Bullet selection**. Simple styles are the most effective. Use the standard bullet generated in the HTML code (the language used to write Web pages) and avoid using custom icons that can appear too cute or flashy, detracting from the objectivity of the list content.

- **Bullet size.** Size bullets the same as text type or a few points smaller. The size of the dot on the i is too small; the size of the lowercase o is too large.

- **Bullet placement.** Standard HTML code does not provide much control over bullet placement, but if possible, center bullets at the midpoint of lowercase letters (the x-height) on the first line of each entry and one or two spaces in front of the text.

- **Layout.** Align lists on the left vertically but leave the right margin ragged, or unjustified.

- **White space.** Add extra line space above, below, or to the sides of a Web list to help separate it from other text or graphics.

- **Color.** A little extra color can be an asset but too many colors cause visual confusion. The safest bet is to stick to black for the type used in the content, with a single second color used for bullets or headline type. Background color use is tricky, as this may vary considerably depending on the settings of the monitors used for viewing. In general, the goal of any added color use is to add contrast between text and background, making the contents easier to read.

Slide Bullets

In modern business and academic environments, digital media have largely replaced overhead transparencies and 35mm slides for group presentations. These days, most group presentations rely on their digital equivalents, projections created from Microsoft's PowerPoint, Apple's Keynote, or similar software. These software programs allow users to quickly create slide presentations from scratch or import content from existing digital documents.

The ease of use of these tools, however, comes at a price. The first is predictability: when everybody uses the same tools, the results increasingly reflect the same, bland choices. Affordability, ease of use, and standardized templates reduce visual uniqueness.

The second downside is overuse. For the same reasons stated above, more and more public gatherings have turned into PowerPoint-intensive displays. Digital slide show formats are now commonplace in executive boardrooms, team activities, college lecture halls, and military briefing rooms. Students in public schools are also increasingly using PowerPoint as a format for reports and homework.

In this atmosphere, slide show use must be carefully managed and appropriately designed in order to attract and maintain audience interest, and be a distinctive and effective communications tool. The use of bullets and lists — a significant part of this use — should also be thoughtfully designed to make the maximum use of the medium.

Key elements necessary for effective use of lists in digital slide presentations:

• Simple, structured layouts.

• Concise, descriptive language.

- Limited use of type fonts.
- Limited use of color.
- Strong color contrasts.
- Short lists and short list entries.

Most of the same visual rules that improve the attractiveness and effectiveness of print documents can be applied for a projected equivalent. But over-dependence on preset templates — both within the slide programs and when importing content from other applications — can diminish the impact, more likely because of choices that are too decorative for their intended audience.

Writing style has special consequences in this format, as almost all of the content in slide presentations depends on headlines, phrases, bulleted lists, and graphic elements such as diagrams and charts. This is not an environment where full sentences and paragraphs thrive, placing more pressure on writers to summarize, condense, and be concise.

Because slide presentations can easily become over-reliant on bulleted lists, look for other ways to display content. This includes migrating list content to charts, re-structuring it as graphs or diagrams, and varying list use with quotations or other extracted text.

Guidelines for the use of bullets and list entries in slide presentations:

- **Type selection.** Keep it simple, Times Roman or Georgia for serif; Arial or Tahoma for sans serif. Georgia and Tahoma were designed for maximum readability on computer monitors, something to keep in mind if a presentation will also be used on a Web site.
- **Type size.** Text is typically 28 to 32 points, with the

major slide presentation programs already preset with a similar point size as defaults. Use smaller size if necessary to hold entries to a single line, but keep the same size for all list text in a presentation. Smaller type size can also be used for credit lines and sources.

- **Type style.** Use normal type and avoid italics, bold, underlining, or all caps except in heads. Just as with printed documents, excessive use of these styles diminishes readability and produces cluttered-looking slides.

- **Line spacing.** If most list entries are only one line in length, keep spacing at the preset "1 line" spacing option provided in slide presentation programs, or 4 to 6 points more than the type size. For longer entries, add extra space between entries. Too much space between lines diminishes readability.

- **Bullet selection.** Simple styles are the most effective. Use the • or ■ and avoid the temptation to use cute or fanciful alternatives.

- **Bullet size.** Size bullets the same as text type or a few points smaller. The size of the dot on the i is too small; the size of the lowercase o is too large.

- **Bullet placement.** Center bullets at the midpoint of lowercase letters (the x-height) on the first line of each entry and one or two spaces in front of the text (this space cannot be adjusted if using the "bullets and numbering" menu option).

- **Layout.** Align lists on the left vertically but leave the right margin ragged, or unjustified. Justified type, when magnified on slides, often looks awkward and can be harder to read.

- **White space**. One list per slide. Center the list on the slide with equal amounts of white space above and below.

- **Sequencing**. For long lists or to add emphasis to any list, format the list to appear one item at a time. PowerPoint automates this option through the Slideshow/Custom Animation menu option.

- **Color**. A little extra color is an asset but too many colors cause visual confusion. The safest bet is one second color only, used for the bullets or the head-line type. If a background color is used, make sure there is plenty of visual contrast between the type and the background. Avoid using white type on dark backgrounds.

Multiple Choice

In the modern office environment, software standards increasingly allow content to be used in more than one format after it is created. A list that first appears in a print document may also be used on a Web site or slide presentation, and vice versa.

Yet just because a few keystrokes can turn an existing document into a slide presentation, the visual results may not match the expectations. Laser printing has different characteristics than type displayed on a screen; a slide presentation projected in a large room looks different than when displayed on a laptop screen.

At best, the text itself will still be readable in any of these format shifts without additional manipulation. At worst, however, visual chaos can result because type fonts are different from one system to the other or program variations cause on-the-fly layout changes. If you do not have control over every format used for a document, minimize disruptive results by using only commonly-available typefaces and simple layouts. To minimize any such potential changes, check in advance by viewing the content in different applications.

Luckily, the efficiencies of personal computers and software make altering lists for different formats relatively simple. Work that has been created in a word processor can easily be imported or pasted into a slide show presentation and design changes managed with templates or style sheet shortcuts.

Another option is the use of the Personal Document Format (pdf) provided with Adobe Acrobat, or a similar cross-platform standard. These applications "lock in" a single, consistent image for a document, maintaining the type and layout in a variety of uses, including laser printouts and Web sites.

Resources
Writing Style

The Dictionary of Concise Writing. Robert Hartwell Fiske. Marion Street Press, Inc., 2002.

The Elements of Style. William Strunk, Jr., and E.B. White. Allyn & Bacon, 2000.

The Elements of Typographic Style. Robert Bringhurst. Hartley & Marks, 2000.

Plain Language (U.S. government guide to writing style). www.plainlanguage.gov

Writing for the Information Age. Bruce Ross-Larson. W.W. Norton & Company, 2002.

Type/Document Design/Computer Interface

Association Typographique Internationale. Redhill, Surrey, United Kingdom. 44-0-1737-780-150. www.atypi.org.

Human Factors & Ergonomics Society (Santa Monica, CA) 310-394-1811. www.hfes.org.

International Reading Association (Newark, DE). 302-731-1600. www.reading.org.

Microsoft Typography. Web site covering issues involved with type usage on the Internet. www.microsoft.com/typography/default.asp.

SIGCHI (Special Interest Group on Computer-Human Interaction/Association for Computing Machinery). www.sigchi.org.

U&lc Online/International Typeface Corporation (Wilmington, MA). 866-823-5828. www.itcfonts.com/ulc.

Usability News. Software Usability Research Lab, Department of Psychology, Wichita State University (Wichita, Kansas). wsupsy.psy.twsu.edu/surl/usabilitynews.

Usability Professionals' Association (Bloomington, IL). 630-980-4997. www.upassoc.org.

Bibliography

"Applying Writing Guidelines to Web Pages." John Morkes and Jakob Nielson. Useit.com, January 6, 1998.

"Assessing Business Proposals: Genre Conventions and Audience Response in Document Design." Luuk Lagerwerf and Ellis Bossers. *The Journal of Business Communication*, October, 2002.

"Attention: An Information Design Perspective." Rune Pettersson. International Institute for Information Design, July, 1999, presentation.

"Composing Letters with Computer-Based Text Editors." J. Gould. *Human Factors*, 1981, 23(5).

"Concise, Scannable, and Objective: How to Write for the Web." J. Morkes, and J. Nielsen. *Alertbox* electronic newsletter, 1997.

"Designing Better Documents: Information Design Professionals Attempt to Understand What Makes Documents Usable and to Apply That Knowledge in Preparing Functional Documents and Records." Saul Carliner. *Information Management Journal*, September 10, 2002.

"Electronic Typeface Readability." Anne White and Antonio Guadarrama. Education Technology/San Diego State University, Fall, 2001, investigation report.

"Finding Information on the Web: Does the Amount of Whitespace Really Matter?" Michael Bernard, Barbara Chaparro, and R. Thomasson. *Usability News* electronic newsletter, 2.1, 2000.

"How to Limit Clinical Errors in Interpretation of Data." Patricia Wright, Carel Jansen, and Jeremy C. Wyatt. *The Lancet*, November 7, 1998.

Human Factors and Typography for More Readable Programs. Ronald M. Baecker. Addison-Wesley Publishing Company, 1990.

"Keeping an Eye on the Text: Some Aspects of Eye Movements and Discourse Processing." Max Louwerse. Poster presentation at the Society for Text and Discourse, Univeristy of Utrecht, The Netherlands, 1997.

"Interface Design and Optimization of Reading of Continuous Text."

Paul Mute. *Cognitive Aspects of Electronic Text Processing*, Ablex Publishing Corporation, 1996.

"Letter Legibility and Visual Word Recognition." Tatjana Nazir, Arthur Jacobs, and J. Kevin O'Regan. *Memory & Cognition*, 1998, 26 (4).

"Rate of Comprehension of an Existing Teleprinter Output and Possible Alternatives." E.C. Poulton and C.H. Brown. *Journal of Applied Psychology*, 1968, 52:16-21.

"A Reading Comprehension Formula of Reader and Text Characteristics." Jaan Mikk and Jaanus Elts. *Journal of Quantitative Linguistics*, 1999, Vol. 6.

"Readability of Fonts in the Windows Environment." Thomas S. Tullis, Jennifer L. Boynton, and Harry Hersh. Association for Computing Machinery, 1995 conference proceedings.

"Reading Online News: A Comparison of Three Presentation Formats." Ryan Baker, Michael Bernard, and Shannon Riley. *Usability News*, 2002, 4.2.

"The Readability of Typefaces and the Subsequent Mood or Emotion Created in the Reader." John E. Gump. *Journal of Education for Business*, May/June 2001.

"Readability of Websites with Various Foreground/Background Color Combinations, Font Types and Word Styles." Alyson L. Hill. Proceedings of the Eleventh National Conference in Undergraduate Research, 1997.

"Stanford-Poynter Project." Research program. The Poynter Institute, 2000.

"A Study of the Readability of On-Screen Text." Eric Weisenmiller. Virginia Polytechnic Institute, graduate thesis, July, 1999.

"Text Width and Margin Width Influences on Readability of GUIs." Melissa Youngman and Dr. Lauren Scharff. Southwestern Psychological Association, 1998, project presentation.

"Web Design: An Empiricist's Guide." Mary Evans. University of Washington, Spring, 1998, project report.

"What's the Best Way to Wrap Links?" Kelly Spain. *Usability News*, 1999, 1.1.

Index